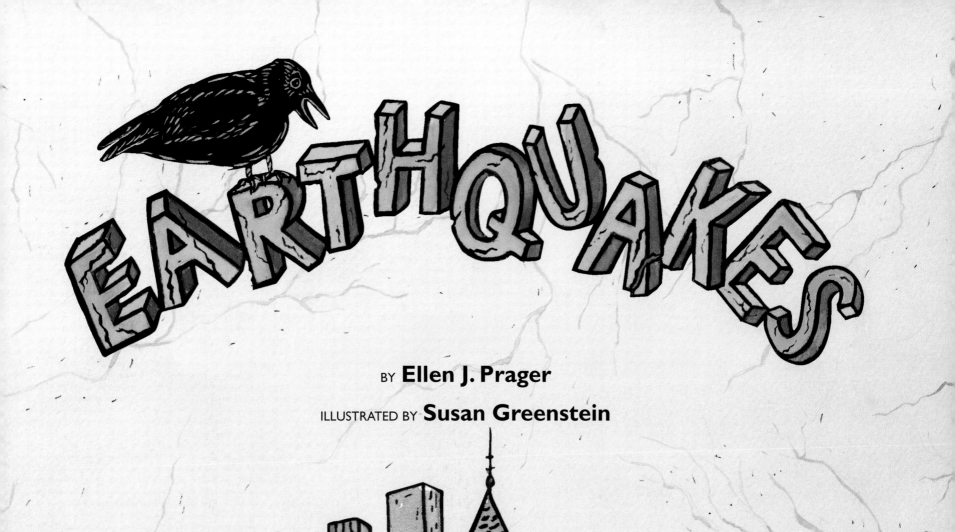

EARTHQUAKES

BY **Ellen J. Prager**

ILLUSTRATED BY **Susan Greenstein**

NATIONAL GEOGRAPHIC SOCIETY

WASHINGTON, D.C.

To all those who have dedicated their lives to earthquake research, education, preparation, and rescue in the aftermath of disaster. —EJP

For my wonderful family, Phil, my husband, and Gina, my daughter, who both help me to see what is special about each day. —SG

SHAKE, RATTLE, AND ROLL...
Buildings, trees, and the ground sway when the Earth gives way.

EARTHQUAKE!

Earthquakes happen on Earth every day. Most are small—too small to feel. But at least once a week, there is a strong earthquake somewhere on the planet.

A strong earthquake can mean disaster for people who live nearby. The ground shakes, jumps, and rolls while people run for safety. Buildings may crack or crumble. Roads can be ripped apart.

What causes an earthquake?

Earthquakes happen when rocks inside the land or under the sea break apart. Rocks can break when they are squeezed, stretched, or pulled in different directions.

Rocks break sort of like a rubber band that has been stretched too far. If the rocks are stretched, squeezed, or pulled too much, they split apart—then snap back slightly out of place.

When rocks break, lots of energy is released. Where does the energy go?

Breaking rocks send energy into the ground. The energy causes the ground to move in what we call an earthquake. To a person, an earthquake can feel like shaking, a sudden jolt, or a slow roll. An earthquake can last for just a few short seconds or go on for several very long minutes.

Most earthquakes happen because Earth's outer surface is moving. Like a huge jigsaw puzzle, the planet's outer surface is made up of big pieces called plates. These plates move very slowly in different directions, so slowly you can't feel them moving. Over time, the plates slide, slip, and bump into each other along their edges.

Pacific Plate

Most earthquakes happen along the edges of Earth's big plates.

Look at the map showing earthquake activity. Can you name two places where earthquakes happen most often?

EARTHQUAKES

Pacific Ocean

San Andreas Fault
CLOSE-UP VIEW

Earthquakes are common in California, especially along the famous San Andreas Fault. Two of Earth's big plates meet at the San Andreas Fault. These two plates move in different directions. Over time, the rocky edges of the two plates bump and stick together, slowly stretching and pulling. Every once in a while, the rocky edges break, release energy, and cause earthquakes.

San Francisco

CALIFORNIA

Los Angeles

Pacific
Ocean

San Andreas Fault

In an earthquake, the ground may move up, down, or sideways. Sideways motion is very dangerous because it can cause tall buildings to sway back and forth or weak houses to collapse. In areas where earthquakes are common, people are learning how to build homes and buildings that will stay safe when the ground moves.

In places where the ground is made of soft sand, shaking can cause buildings to sink down and tumble over. Where earthquakes happen, buildings and homes should be specially designed and be built on solid ground.

FORESHOCK

24

Sometimes there are many small earthquakes before the big one. These are called foreshocks. After the big earthquake—the mainshock—again there may be many small quakes. These are called aftershocks.

MAINSHOCK

AFTERSHOCK

EARTHQUAKE SAFETY

1. Stay calm during an earthquake.

2. If outside, find an open space away from power poles, buildings, fences, etc.

3. If inside, stay away from windows. Take cover under a sturdy desk, table, or door frame.

4. Listen for instructions from a teacher or parent, or listen to the radio for information.

No one has found a sure way to predict earthquakes, so the best protection is to be prepared and know what to do. Find a safe place and stay away from things that could come crashing down.

We cannot prevent
earthquakes from
happening. Earthquakes
are part of Earth's
changing nature.

Scientists study earthquakes to learn more about them and to help prevent injury and damage. One day we may be able to predict earthquakes and give people more warning.

Have you ever felt an earthquake?

Create your own earthquake

Here's what you'll need:

- **A square or rectangular baking pan**
- **Enough sand to fill the pan about halfway**
- **A brick or a fist-size flat rock**

1. Place the sand in the baking pan and pack it down so that the surface is smooth and flat.

2. Place the brick or rock on the sand. Does it stay on top of the sand or sink?

3. Now shake the pan back and forth.

What happens?

The brick or rock now sinks into the sand or falls over!

What did you discover? (use a mirror to read)

You were the earthquake. If the brick or rock had been a house built on loose sand, the house would have sunk into the ground. Walls might have cracked, and rooms might have collapsed. In places where earthquakes are likely to happen, buildings should be built on solid ground and follow strict safety codes.

To create her paintings, Susan Greenstein used black ink
and watercolor paint on watercolor paper.

Book design by LeSales Dunworth
Text is set in Gill Sans. Display text is set in Dirtyhouse, and some is hand-lettered.

Jump Into Science series consultant: Gary Brockman, Early Education Science Specialist

Earthquake safety tips adapted from *National Geographic World* article:
"With a Jolt: Earthquakes Shatter Houses—and Lives," by David George Gordon, January 1998.

Library of Congress Cataloging-in-Publication Data
Prager, Ellen J.
Earthquakes / by Ellen J. Prager ; illustrated by Susan Greenstein.
p. cm. — (Jump into science)
ISBN 0-7922-8202-7
1. Earthquakes—Juvenile literature. [1. Earthquakes.] I. Greenstein,
Susan, ill. II. Title. III. Series.
QE521.3 .P727 2002
551.22—dc21
2001000686

Printed in Mexico

The world's largest nonprofit scientific and educational organization, the National Geographic Society was founded in 1888 "for the increase and diffusion of geographic knowledge." Since then it has supported scientific exploration and spread information to its more than eight million members worldwide. The National Geographic Society educates and inspires millions every day through magazines, books, television programs, videos, maps and atlases, research grants, the National Geographic Bee, teacher workshops, and innovative classroom materials. The Society is supported through membership dues, charitable gifts, and income from the sale of its educational products. Members receive NATIONAL GEOGRAPHIC magazine—the Society's official journal—discounts on Society products and other benefits. For more information about the National Geographic Society, its educational programs and publications, and ways to support its work, please call 1-800-NGS-LINE (647-5463) or write to the following address:

NATIONAL GEOGRAPHIC SOCIETY
1145 17th Street N.W.
Washington, D.C. 20036-4688
U.S.A.
Visit the Society's Web site: www.nationalgeographic.com